Approaching Ice

Also by Elizabeth Bradfield

Interpretive Work

Approaching Ice

poems

Elizabeth Bradfield

A KAREN & MICHAEL BRAZILLER BOOK
PERSEA BOOKS / NEW YORK

Persea Books, Inc.
853 Broadway
New York, NY 10003

Bradfield, Elizabeth.
Approaching ice : poems / Elizabeth Bradfield. — 1st ed.
    p. cm.
"A Karen & Michael Braziller book."
Includes bibliographical references and index.
ISBN 978-0-89255-355-6 (original trade pbk. : alk. paper)
1. Arctic regions–Poetry. 2. Polar regions–Poetry. I. Title.
PS3602.R3396A77 2009
811'.6--dc22

                    2009030439

Designed by nördliche
First edition
Printed in the United States of America

Contents

I

Polar Explorer Capt. John Cleves Symmes (1820)   3

In the Polar Regions   4

A Grim Place for Ponies   5

Wilson's Specimens   7

— Notes on Ice in *Bowditch*   8

Thoughts on Early Arctic Explorers

    and Your Time in Churchill   9

Polar Explorer James Weddell (1822)   12

Tourists in Antarctica   14

Polar Explorer Carsten Borchgrevink (1895, 1899)   15

Phrenology   17

Polar Explorer Jules Sébastien César Dumont d'Urville (1840)   19

Invention   21

Legacy   22

Emissary   24

— Notes on Ice in *Bowditch*   25

It Began With Reading of Antarctic Adventures   26

Polar Explorer Salomon August Andrée (1897)   27

Polar Autumn   29

The Third Reich Claims Neu Schwabenland   30

Polar Explorer Adrien de Gerlache,

    First to Winter Below the Antarctic Circle (1898)   33

— Notes on Ice in *Bowditch*   35

Bowditch as First Discovery, First Exploration   36

Polar Explorer Matthew Henson,
    Assistant to Admiral Peary (1909)   37
Against Solitude   39
Polar Explorer Douglas Mawson Accomplishes
    the South Magnetic Pole (1909)   40
Why They Went   42
Polar Explorer Apsley Cherry-Garrard (1911)   43
In Preparation   45

II

On the Longing of Early Explorers   49
Polar Explorer Nobu Shirase's Five Rules (1911)   50
First Austral Contact   53
— Notes on Ice in *Bowditch*   55
Snow Goggles: Whalebone and Sinew   56
Icebound   57
Polar Explorer Robert Falcon Scott (1912)   59
In Praise of Entropy   61
Arctos/Antarktikos   62
En Route   64
Polar Explorer Frank Hurley, Photographer
    on Shackleton's *Endurance* Expedition (1915)   65
Song of the Ice Breaker Prow   67
Polar Explorer Ernest Shackleton (1922)   68
Fine-Tuning   70

— Notes on Ice in *Bowditch*   71

Polar Explorer Louise Arner Boyd (1924)   72

Roughnecks and Rakes One and All,
     the Poet Speaks to Her Subjects, Polar Explorers   74

Polar Explorer Donald B. MacMillan Brings
     Color Film to the Arctic (1925)   76

Wives of the Polar Explorers   78

Polar Explorer Richard Evelyn Byrd (1933)   80

WYSSA   82

— Notes on Ice in *Bowditch*   83

Admundsen in Nome   84

On Ground Tracked by Wolf, Snowshoe,
     Sled, Ski, and Snowmachine   85

Polar Explorer John Forbes Nash, Jr.,
     Self-Declared Emperor of Antarctica (1967)   86

Why Shackleton's Stories Are Being Retold in Book and Film   88

Lady: Polar Explorer and Last
     of the Enderby Island Cattle (1993)   89

They Called it Nukey-Poo   91

— Notes on Ice in *Bowditch*   92

Vicarious   93

Polar Explorer Lynne Cox (2002)   95

NOTES   99

BIBLIOGRAPHY   100

ACKNOWLEDGMENTS   101

I

Because this life, this alarm clock time card
percolator direct deposit income tax stop light

seems vast and blank and numbing.

Tell me secret orchids hide
between the black rock and the ice.

Tell me a wild bird sings deep
in the crevasses, wingstrokes cracking air.

Tell me there's a surface we can walk on
lidding miles of plumed and luminescent fish.

I'm ready to be amazed. I'm longing for it.

Polar Explorer Capt. John Cleves Symmes (1820)

Outside his Cincinnati windows, a street game in full swing.
Some kid shouts *Safe!* Another jeers *Symmes' hole!*

A fight breaks out. Inside, Symmes keeps pressing
his human face against the frozen wall of what

is known, not seeing through but melting into it
his own features, his own strange form. He wanted

explanations for the plenty at the poles:
caribou twice the size of white-tailed deer,

white bears dwarfing black, schools of herring
that return each year fat and flashing, more fish

than ever could fit into an ice-choked ocean.
Shouldn't the north be barren? Wouldn't the cold...

Hope effervesced in him, bubbled toward utopia. *Americus*,
he'd say to his son, *there is more to discover*

and we'll be patron to it. It could almost pass
for science—the icy ring and sloping verge

that he proposed, a concavity, a hole four thousand
miles across at the globe's north end, and,

for symmetry, six thousand at the south, another earth
within our earth, more perfect, richer, the borealis

streaming from it like a neon sign.

In the Polar Regions

Long from home. Glaciers capping the hills
like false teeth. It's not just the odd meat
we're carving, clawed flippers and flightless
wings, or the long-churned distance to any news of home,
any first-born or failing parent. There
are other signs this place is foreign. The ship
converses with ice packed around it, groans
and squeaks, an occasional outraged crack.

It takes a particular man for this, you know,
able to be short-sighted for months on end.
The air is constantly aluminum with snow,
and my mouth, too, tastes of metal. Salt
of iron seeping from my weakened gums.
Each morning, I pack drift around my tongue
to freeze the soft flesh holding my teeth.

It all goes to slush—ground underneath
our tents, my mouth, the knack for conversation.
Walking west, five of us have fallen
to dangle alongside cliffs of ice, the thin crust
breaking into chasm easily, as if such sudden transformations
were to be expected and we're the fools to be surprised.
Only a thin rope holds us to the surface. Hanging,
there's nothing to do but stare at the blue contours of freeze
and tongue our loosening teeth, test the stringy roots
that hold them, wait for a tug from the ones left above.

A Grim Place for Ponies

South Pole Expedition, 1910

The men wrap burlap over splitting hooves
and rig wide shoes to fool the ice. The men
fill diaries with haunch and hoof,
quirks and favorites. With frostbit hands
the men brush their ponies twice daily.
Stroke and groom.

*Punch, Nobby, Guts, Blücher, Blossom,
Jimmy Pigg, Weary Willie, Uncle Bill*

Nightly, the men hack shelters in snow
to protect them. Which are nightly
bucked down
                              then rebuilt as tents fray.

*I must say that the abandoning of the ponies
was the one thing that had never entered my head.
Their implicit trust in us was touching to behold.*

Misplaced, mis-engineered and miscast
as steeds for these knights—or so
the men imagine themselves, trudging
toward a goal found only by magic,
lodestone bowing to earth's nadir—

it's the ponies that pull this tale,
make these blusterers attendants:

*The poor beast was barely able to struggle out
of the holes it made as it plunged forward.*

Choose only white ones, Scott ordered.
But what do ponies know of Empire and the National
Effort? Of stiff upper lip and steely jaw?

Guts himself had gone, and a dark streak of water alone
showed the place where the ice had opened under him.

Braided tails brittle with ice. Tack tattering
in katabatic winds. Ideas of care were rent.

Poor trustful creatures! Getting the pick I struck
where Titus told me.

Feed bag now lining boots. Flank meat
for stew. A mound of snow
blown over the remains.

Wilson's Specimens

Quickly, he learned the art of flensing,
of peeling back the strange skins
from the swimming birds that streaked beneath
the *Terra Nova*'s prow,
                                   learned
a rhythm of slice and pause timed
to the ship's lurch, bright flash
of metal in his chill hand conducted
by wave and ice against hull.

And so the skins piled up—became his plenty
as onions dwindled in the barrels and flour sacks
sagged from full and the taste of his own mouth
became foreign to him.
                                   Black and white pelts
feathered, sleek, unqualified by gray. His diary
of the journey. His best calendar of days
—moldy, cramped in their salted boxes—
but, once home, exotic, redolent
of all he found he could not say.

ice. *Frozen water, the solid form of H$_2$O.*

Basic. Describing nothing of its colors. Nothing of its cold. Of its different densities and the hard process of freezing. But perhaps a good beginning.

ice anchor. *An anchor designed for securing a vessel to ice.*

Treachery inherent in the dig of metal flukes, the initial crack of contact.   Uncertain mooring that could be drifting, that could break

into drift.

ice atlas. *A publication containing a series of ice charts showing geographic distribution of ice, usually by seasons or months.*

Not a bad idea. Can they make one for the climate of the heart?

ice-blink. *A whitish glare on low clouds above an accumulation of distant ice.*

Endless metaphor, this state, for love or destiny, I'd be no good at spotting this. Each time, I'd convince myself the pale was imagined. That my eyes, blinking to clear, were playing tricks. That the horizon was free of impediments.

ice-bound. *Adj. Pertaining to a harbor, inlet, etc. when entry or exit is prevented by ice, except possibly with the assistance of an ice-breaker.*

There are always crashing exceptions. Here, each revved-up push leaves a bit of paint, flaked toxin, maybe a weakening of steel in exchange. There is never only one thing being hit.

ice boundary. *The demarcation at any given time between fast ice and pack ice or between areas of pack ice of different concentrations. See also* ICE EDGE.

Any boundary wanders, sweetheart. Definition to definition.

Thoughts on Early Arctic Explorers and Your Time in Churchill

Come back safely with all your gloves
intact and your rolls of slide film finished.
Come back with your glasses unbroken, my love,
your desire for ice and ringed seal quenched.

You've pointed out enough ptarmigan,
hidden but for their black eyes in the drifts.
You've lectured enough to the curious, let them
go to the library for information, lift

excuses for travel from others' tales
of *what I learned* in chasing restlessness,
in staring at a cub in snow, its pale
fur whorled and mussed, imagination pointless.

They've paid your way to see freeze-up
on Hudson Bay, the limestone pools inset
with Precambrian shell, the traps laid out to nab
bears that stray too close to town for comfort.

You've treated frost nip, suggested shutter speeds.
You've given them enough. Return to me.

Enough. Think of the historic hardships.
Cold, tired, fruit a distant memory—
and the body's envelope loosens, skin sloughing
from the face's planes. This is the grip

of the poles. It pulls apart your layers,
the glues that make you whole. The white of it,
the chill, the silence that's so strangely lit
by the oscillating sun—all failures

here are dramatic. Those of light
of body or of will. The vast cold
isolates your small, red pulse
and runs thoughts wild as dogs at night,
tricks your flesh into quitting. Fingers, earlobes
only the first of you to become useless.

First, be stoic. Take the chill between
your teeth and grip it. Frame each mirage
with logic, and if rendered blind don't seethe,
just pack your sockets with cocaine to assuage

the sharp ache. Document your madness.
Take the brunt of the sled's weight even when
you are exhausted. Quote Keats into the relentless
wind. Blake to your companions in the thin

shell of your tent. Devonshire, yes, and Surrey.
These are real places to which you can return.
Not the odd, directionless roads you follow, asplay
across the tundra, unmapped, unplanned, lain

by glacial river. Even on the ice
you are yourself. Raised to venture and return.

You return having learned terms like *Krummholz Effect*—
trees scoured to the weather side, not a limb
pointing north to the wind's source. Flimsy
twigs reach east and west. And the horizon

is wide and shimmering, without scale, your eyes
unused to such long twilight, its scrim
across the day. Gore-Tex, Thinsulate, skin
under engineered layers. Zeiss,

Nikon, Olympus. Glass eyes held before
your eyes in attempts to safely truncate
distances, make them closer, more

familiar. To bring back something polar.
Of course no film can translate the cold, light,
or bone-deep sense of supervised terror.

Polar Explorer James Weddell (1822)

When the year's new ice is four inches thin,
their long incisors cut toward air. By spring the walls rise up
six feet, almost their length. *Leptonychotes weddellii.* Furthest south
of any seal to pup, they use the frozen sea itself
as nursery, chewing holes to move from suckle to hunt.
Put your ear to ice and you'll hear their improbable,
space-age trilling. Their songs of claim.

How is legacy achieved? Weddell named nothing
after himself, not sea, not the seal which barely registers
in his accounts. The sea, now his, he called George IV.

A spawning ground for polar ice,
it crushed de Gerlache's *Antarctic.* Crushed
the famed *Endurance.* All winter it grinds clockwise,
seizing and milling what's trapped, releasing
tabular bergs large enough—the size of Rhode Island!—
to make news even here. And why did Weddell venture

there? The profit of seals hauled out
on the rocky Orkneys and Shetlands but also this:
a hazed set of dots seen once in 1762
and never again—the Aurora Islands.

They are still undiscovered. But Weddell
found his strange fame. One hundred years,
he held the title *furthest south* and held it
without tragedy. Turning back before turning back was faint
hope or escape thrilling and legend.

He died as many of the southbound did:
in the city he launched from, poor and alone.

And the sea keeps cracking, keeps circling
its confines, creating more ephemeral islands
perforated by the breath holes of sleek-headed
seals, which were never worth much and so never
hunted to dramatic loss, and so less known.

We've tried to bring them north
for education, for entertainment, but
they chew into the concrete walls that hold them
and die of infected teeth.

Tourists in Antarctica

To strain for communion
with the air, the seals, the memory
of whalers and explorers gone
is exhausting. Impossible to wander off
and find some proxy-tree
to dally underneath. Balked
at every turn by rules and the stern
insistence of climate and its weather.

But you've grown to love the orange
suit you clamber into daily, the firm
hold of goggles on your skull,
halogen lights in the long, long twilight.
You understand, of course, dissatisfaction and yearning
for its opposite are what this place
has always held.

Polar Explorer Carsten Borchgrevink
(1895, 1899)

A generally useful hand
on the Norwegian *Antarctic*,
Borchgrevink sets foot
on Cape Adare.
                    No guess-work
of pot shards or chipped flint
to confirm this first landing
on the continent. Log books
and diaries in languages still living
document it.

                    Four years pass. Borchgrevink
returns, sets up a hut and shed,
stocks it with socks, tins of peas,
tobacco. He stays the winter
with ten men and 75 dogs. He dines
on penguins that, in the course
of their wanderings, arrive. This

is the sole record we have
of a continent's first human
habitation.
                    But what slim hold
history has even here. Our countable
arrivals set against beaches cobbled
with seals, half a million birds
in this spot at breeding,
thunderheads of krill.

Along the thin walls that held
the men that winter, Adélies have continued
to gather and nest and shit,
raising their young.
                    And so
the oldest building on Antarctica
is nearly ruined, nearly buried
in guano, nearly overwritten with sound
and stink, with the fertile plenty
of unrecorded lives
going on.

Phrenology

Were the earth a skull, the lump
at its base would read to Victorian
doctors as *amativeness*: connubial
love, procreative lust. And where the peninsula

stretches up toward Patagonia
a smidge of *philoprogenitiveness*,
parental love, a fondness for pets
and the generally helpless. Jules Dumont d'Urville,

man of his times, had his own skull mapped
before sailing to map earth's southern blur.
Were the earth a skull and someone
with knowledge laid hands on it, felt topography

for expression of its psyche, would this
answer what questions are asked
in slog and observation, in sample and ice core?

Sub-Antarctic islands bulge at the spot
of *combativeness*: self-defense, a go-to
disposition and love of debate. *Alimentiveness*
at South Africa and New Zealand: appetite,

an enjoyment of food and drink. Jules
was pleased with what the doctor found,
felt himself seen truly. But what judges
our human descriptions of place?

Weather? Lichens? The transitory animals
that touch upon it? Were the earth a skull
shaped by humors. Were understanding
so palpable, so constant.

Polar Explorer Jules Sébastien César Dumont d'Urville (1840)

For a day he sailed through bergs and along a face
of ice. Land? The bellies of penguins, when slit,
scattered stones on the deck, a granite morse
that said rock grounded what they passed. Adélie Land,
he called it. Named not for patron or ruler
or favored lieutenant, but wife.

...an act of justice, a sort of obligation I have fulfilled
to give her, after losing three children, after his years away,
something *to perpetuate...my deep and lasting gratitude.*

Rock had been his fame before. Twenty years earlier,
in Greece, a farmer showed him a statue of Venus
so beautiful d'Urville had to have it for France.
Dragging her back to the ship, chased
by bandits, her broken arms were left on the rock
of Melos. Her body stands still in the Louvre.

What did he lose to Antarctica? Time. Men
to dysentery and scurvy. The boyhood
of his own boy. I wonder what she thinks of it now,
standing in her climate-controlled room,
the business of hands taken. I like to think she tracked
his journey and return, heard among visitors
whispers of his end: a train wreck coming home
from a day at Versailles with his wife and son.

The land, the statue are still where he left them,
and each Austral summer his wife's other namesake,

a penguin, hunts up stones for its nest,
presents them to a mate, steals more
from other nests and then, until the chick
fledges, guards them as if rightful.

Invention

It was prompted by winds directionless
and all-directioned, by fingers
clumsy in thick shadows cast
by penguin-oil lamps, and by men
scrabbling the ground, sifting bits of skin

and hairs loosed from boot or bag
to find what had been dropped
in making the evening's comfort: tea.
Mawson, legend has it, took his ration
and put it in a sock. Such a simple trick.

Unnecessary in parlor or ceremony,
but here, shaking leaves from a tin
as wind twists snow up from the tent floor,
a godsend. Before, on each tired march home

they'd squinted, snow blind and stooped,
over old camps, hoping their cast dregs
had not scattered. Now it was easy
to scavenge *the old tea bags at
our old camps as we pass them*. And it must

have been comfort that what they steeped
into weak brew had never been read
loose in the base of a mug, had never
attempted to tell them whether or not
or which of them would return.

Legacy

—for Vitus Bering

They've closed again the gap that you first sailed,
Russian sponsored Dane, so cousins on the Diomedes

are in post Cold War touch. But you made the map

that made the border, sighting lands just guessed at
between Kamchatka and America's west coast. And we
   write history from what's put down *officially*, maps

and logbooks made and kept by the survivors
of your death, of your loss of ambition from years

line-toeing across the forehead of Siberia. Finally you set sail for

glory—or not *for* but *from* whatever pushes us beyond
our birth-spots. What pushes us away? I, too, have left
   for some spot unknown by those who claim me, for

place unhooked from kin and story. I've fled
the watched life of any hometown where if

you kick a dog, infect a girl, break a window

the girl turns out to be your mother's landlord's
cousin, the dog a beat cop's mutt, and shards
   cut your sister's foot: Each chafed-at thing's a window

in your glass-house world. So the age-old lust for places
we pretend are free of consequence. It's the same

now as it was with Oedipus, poor stiff, running to escape his fate

and running smack dab into it, an awful
scene, a nightmare warning we need to keep
   repeating because, of course, fate

never seems immediate. For weeks Bering's crew feasted
on the delicious bulk of sea cows (now extinct).

They played cards, anted up with otter pelts that *promyshlenniki* later

stripped from the shores. Foxes bit the men's toes
at night. The land ate them as they ate the land,
   calling it need, worrying about it later.

Emissary

Right now my poems are crossing
Drake Passage on a boat named for the boat
that, arguably, started it all:
Cook's *Endeavour*. From which he saw
the continent. I am at home.

In the usual chair. And she
who draws the map of my life
in stranger lines than I can key
carries them in her bag, a bridge
between speechlessness and speech.

It seems right, invented as they were
in her months gone on other ships, to
other shores. I wish them well and hope
that there, echoing against the ice, they sound
both true and strange.

Notes on Ice in *Bowditch*

ice breccia. *Ice pieces of different age frozen together.*
Patchwork sewn tight with freeze into one big blanket. The old, old blue with the new white. Different strengths and ways of being brittle. This is my answer to the years between us. There can be fusing. There is a name for it.

ice bridge. *1. Surface river of ice of sufficient thickness to impede or prevent navigation. 2. An area of fast ice between the mainland and nearby inhabited islands used in winter as a means of travel.*
Barrier and pathway. It's love that makes me so full of fury, so unable to be tender.

ice buoy. *A sturdy buoy, usually a metal spar, used to replace a more easily damaged buoy during a period when heavy ice is anticipated.*
The key is in the anticipating, shoring up for season or storm. The key, really, is that the million million things to be anticipated can't. Even sturdier objects will be battered.

ice cake. *Any relatively flat piece of sea ice less than 20 meters across.*
Serve this on my birthday, would you? Frosted with hoar and lit by beacons so ships won't crash upon it.

ice canopy. *From the point of view of the submariner.*
Always a point of view. But try and rig this up for my birthday also, over the ice cake, sky filtering through, refracting. And indicating by its very presence that we must be drowning.

It Began With Reading of Antarctic Adventures

Half an hour with coffee
marking up a book—a check
to note sense, exclamation mark at astonishment
or disbelief, pages heavy on my knees.

And then a day of my own
work-related hazards. Tempestuous
blizzard of keys, avalanche of
email. Eye strain at the screen's glare. Chair creak
like something about to give way.

Snow fell. The street was plowed and salted.
My dreams were white and treacherous.
I walked as if the pavement's grooves
were signs of where it could collapse.
I wanted it to.

Polar Explorer Salomon August Andrée (1897)

O, terrible—silence over ice—
no panting dogs, no hissing runners,
no footfall to break it. Just the crack
and groan of its own awful straining
rising up.

You warm your hands at the flame
that lifts you. The balloon's silk
is a second sun, unsetting. You're always in its noon,
directly underneath its rippling light.

There's a red smear on one floe, white
bear loping away from the seal's meat.
There's a quick spout in a lead,
the whale's back there, gone.

When blizzards, no ground to fix
your boots to, just directionless swirl
and the compass' doubtful arrow.

Who else has breathed air this clear, crystals of it
hardening briefly in your lungs? Who else has so brightly
risen above the dangerous landscape?

And when you find that you are losing height,
when the earth calls you down to its own slogging,
when it's been decided that you've traveled long enough
as ghosts, silent and apart, you know

some disaster of hunger and cold awaits
      —your bones' location to be a mystery for thirty years—
you know your limbs may no longer have the knack
of pulling, of recovery, of resistance, and you're glad anyway
to be mortal again, and stumbling.

Polar Autumn

The twilight upon twilight,
the letters written and amended
and added to, then sealed
in the mailbag, shut to their
continuing, as if, once inside,
they would begin arriving.
Layers drifting up.

Months of this.

Dove-wing sky, unshadowed land—
or perhaps, rather than unshadowed,
all blurred to shade. Even the dreamers,
the romantics who linger at day's edge, casting
back to sleep, forward to obligation,
even they are unmoored in the drifting
drifting light.

The Third Reich Claims Neu Schwabenland

Antarctica, 1939

I.

Ice is not land, so how to claim it? How to mark it owned
        without thatched roofs, artifacts from conquered tribes, quaint
                yeomen tilling non-native crops on the annexed shore?
The planes *Passat* and *Boreas* were catapulted
        from the chill deck of the *Schwabenland*
           into the frigid, uncharted air
to fly across the ice (one-fifth
        of the continent) and photograph it (11,000 pictures),
           to drop their aluminum darts
tattooed with a crooked cross
        every twenty miles into what they saw
           as if they could fix it, as if
they could pin it fast
        and point to it as theirs
           here   here
anchorages rich with whale oil,
        space on the map of the world
           now called Neu Schwabenland.

II.

On the shelf: skull of a fox, abalone shell,
  bundle of porcupine quills—my mnemonics
   of travel, of what I have discovered.
I buy star BD$^\wedge$-03$^\wedge$5750 online
  and name it Incognita. There's a certificate
   that comes in the mail, a mythology, a map.
Is this dog mine? She has begun,
  some nights, to growl, low and defiant,
   when I move her from the couch, hers.
If my lover leaves me, what will become
  of our photographs and stories,
   who will keep the dog?
I claim the lips of Barb Burzynski
  that night in the woods on Vashon before
   I knew that she was married.

III.

Ice is not land. Is restless. And what was claimed
       has moved, is inching toward sea,
          has maybe broken off,
calved from the frozen edge, and now trails
          its dust and shit and egg shards and abandoned fuel tins,
          trails what stories it held
through the ocean's haloclines
       and thermoclines, its pelagic and benthic layers,
          scattering them across its sea floor.
Maybe by now one of the marked aluminum darts
       tall as an emperor penguin and
          dropped   dropped   dropped
let loose in calculated transects then
       stumbled over, perched on, nested under, scoured
          by wind, maybe scoured of its markings,
thin and pocked, maybe it is settling
       beneath miles of water, is crumpling,
          declarative not of claim, but of time.

Polar Explorer Adrien de Gerlache, First to Winter Below the Antarctic Circle (1898)

What hope at the outset: to put
his small nation in the running. To seek
a pure and scientific aim untroubled
by what his king, Leopold, was seeking
in the Congo.
                    The *Belgica* stuck on purpose?
Too proud to say it was error and pride
that kept them south too long? There were not
enough lamps for the unsunned days.
Not enough bags of flour or books.
They were trapped in pack ice.
                                      North
of them, under the same crown, children
and wives were hostage to rubber. Bodies
dropped in a dark river to become
unrecognizable. Easy, there, to lose flesh to rot.

Under de Gerlache, a man was buried at sea.
They trudged out from the ships's stuck hull,
hauling him on a sledge. They hacked
a grave, opening ice to the sea below
that still moved, teemed, heaved
through the Austral winter.
                              A few short words—
and through them, uneven reports and crackings
as the grave was opened again,
again to the sea.

                    And then he was gone

to them, though his body
would not have gone to bone
quickly, chill allowing his flesh
to crawled by sea spiders
and limpets for years.

So was he erased? And were the bodies
in the river of Africa erased? No
headstones for either but memory. The sea
holds them all now. And in the water all have tongues.

ice cover. *The ratio, expressed in tenths, of the amount of ice to the total area of sea surface in a defined area.*

Chill blanket. Breaking at the sea's restless turning which is not a ratio or an algorhythm. Or, if it is, is too complicated for us to explain with anything as whole as numbers. Nights, one leg always comes bare when you turn. Nights without you, the bed is cold.

ice crystal. *Any one of a number of macroscopic crystalline forms in which ice appears.*

Wear it for a while against the lobe of your ear. The skin will ache in parting, will burn in retaliation. How I hate the sneaky leavetaking of some things, dripping from me even as I hold them.

ice crystals. *A type of precipitation composed of slowly-falling, very small, unbranched crystals of ice which often seem to float in the air. It may fall from a cloud or from a cloudless sky. It is visible only in direct sunlight or an artificial light beam, and does not appreciably reduce visibility. The latter quality helps to distinguish it from ice fog, which is composed largely of droxtals.*

The most ephemeral things require the longest definition. Words settling upon each other, accumulating enough weight for meaning. Explain that slight narrowing of your eyes. Don't try to predict me, tie me to a four-week course of moods. It may fall from a cloud or from a cloudless sky.

ice edge. *The demarcation at any given time between open sea and sea ice of any kind, whether fast or drifting.*

This is where you jump. This is the map-edge that can't be drawn or that must never cease being drawn, the edge that crumbles or that grows new boundaries. This is the demarcation of lovers.

Bowditch as First Discovery, First Exploration

That book, sailor's bible shelved
down in the basement beside the set
of Shakespeare's plays (my mother's).
I was not allowed to turn its pages
unsupervised—so thin,
so delicate and heavy-inked.

I turned always to the star charts:
White scatter on a dark blue circle.
Transparent sheets to story

the scatter with lines. My father
followed these before I was born,
can still recite the Winter Hexagon:
Capella, Aldebaran, Rigel...
I hoped a book would offer pattern
to my own haphazard points.

Polar Explorer Matthew Henson,
Assistant to Admiral Peary (1909)

Muttered in bunks, bent to the capstan's spokes,
nightly whispered after exchange of course and speed
at watch-shift, *What will he look like frostbit? Son*
of the tropics, how will his dark blood
fare?
    But once on the ice, once
our hoods were drawn and hoar had coweled
our features, once my broad nose was hid and Peary's
blue stare shaded—O twilight world we traveled through
again together, all shadow and shadow in the short season
between the constant darkness and the breaking of the frozen sea.

They'll say that, of all his followers, he brought me
to the pole because I could not challenge the fix
he made, bent over a bright pan of mercury, sextant
toward the low, red sun. Or they'll say he wanted
all glory within the parlors. But who can separate
a shadow from what casts it?
                Twenty years my shadow
traveled behind his, and on that last march toward the world's
last goal, mine alone of the crew
                though behind me,
it is almost forgotten, were Egingwah, Seeglo,
Ooqneah, and Ootah, whose words I tongued
as no others of the crew learned to, whose hunts
I joined and dogs I kicked. Let me tell
you, once, far from the iced-in hull, we slew
a bear. And the skin beneath that yellow-white fur was black.

Tell me what is loyalty, what ambition. Tell me how
to best judge a suitable man. Forgotten once the ship
came home, returned to the dim of my life
on cobblestones. Named on certificates, yes,
dutifully, but not invited.
                            Eighty years
before I am dug from my plot in Bronx's Woodlawn and reinterred
in the privileged swales of Arlington, lain beside him
whose burdens I carried those many ventures.
                                              But even as we trudged north
that final time, yoked to our goal, a related story
was beginning: two boys named Anaukaq
ran the tundra, flinging rocks at birds. One with eyes
like winter water, one with hair curled wild beneath his hood, and each
aware of his difference from his brothers.

Against Solitude

Leave your reindeer bag, damp and moldering,
and slide into mine. Two of us, I'm sure, could
warm it, could warm. Let me help you from your traces,
let me rub what's sore. Don't speak. Your hair has grown long
in our march, soft as my wife's. Keep your beard turned
toward the tent's silk, your fusty breath—I know none of us
can help it, I know, and truthfully I'm glad for any scent in this...

Hush. How long has it been since my mouth has held anything
other than ice and pemmican? Your skin, though wan and sour,
is firm, delicious. Yes, your shoulder, your hip. I'd not thought
how soft a man's hip would be, how curved the flesh above the backs
of his thighs—listen. Do you hear the wind moaning, the ice
groaning beneath us as it strains?

Polar Explorer Douglas Mawson
Accomplishes the South Magnetic Pole (1909)

They've been sleeping together in one bag for warmth—
Mawson, Mackay, and David, the professor,
whose every fumbled pocket
sprouts an instrument or gauge.

No dogs, they've hauled
sledges and themselves up Drygalski Glacier
to plateau, searching.

Calculation more than anything of gut or heart
guides them toward the spot where compass arrows
stand on end.

But local deviations—rocks flung down from stars
that hold strange metals—rob the task of its simplicity.

The professor weakens first and soon Mawson will say *It took
the lot of us to make a whole man* (for rhythm
I wish he'd said *one man*, but I am not his
author). Even so, they carry on. And at some point

math and exhaustion tell them
they stand on it—

not the fixed lance of axis,
but the magnetic pull which wanders each year
ten miles or so, shifting. They make a pot of tea.
They take a picture and stare at the trembling
guide in someone's palm.

That's an ending.

But epilogue:

the journey home they almost didn't finish.
The thousand-plus miles they walked in total.
And then, returned from this land

that is more ice than earth and where
bays become headlands in one cold season,
revisiting sightings log and algorhythms, it turns out
they were never there.

Why They Went

*that men might learn what the world is like at the spot
where the sun does not decline in the heavens.*
—*Apsley Cherry-Garrard*

Frost bitten. Snow blind. Hungry. Craving
fresh pie and hot toddies, a whole roasted
unflippered thing to carve. Craving a bed
that had, an hour before entering,
been warmed with a stone from the hearth.

Always back to Eden—to the time when we knew
with certainty that something watched and loved us.
That the very air was miraculous and ours.
That all we had to do was show up.

The sun rolled along the horizon. The light never left them.
The air from their warm mouths became diamonds.
And they longed for everything they did not have.
And they came home and longed again.

Polar Explorer Apsley Cherry-Garrard (1911)

Young thing, eyeglasses constant trouble—
fogging, iced, the metal frame burning
where it touched his temples, magnifying the white
of the whole continent against his eye.

He often gave the lenses up outside shelter,
but what of that? Snow grit blurred everyone's horizon,
the hot burn of blindness threatened every iris,
haze lowered on them all. Three men set out
through polar night toward a thing unseen.

O valiant. Those eggs nested in his mittens,
replacing there his hands, exposed skin turning brittle as shell.
Some strange grail, some strange holy land
of emperors waddling in the months-long dark,
beaks opening to make the air metallic with their calls,
sky above the only signal of their import
with its baffling scrim of green flexing light.

The heavy eggs, the birds they were the first
to ever see huddled inland and waiting
for the hatching, the bright opening that would come
before the sun itself returned; flight's evolution
thought to be encased in their shells.

He carried them back, good scientist, through all the usual travails
made polar—weakness, hunger, doubt. He left some bird
with a stone of ice warming on the nest of its uplifted toes,
the stone-sized egg in his hand,
a trick that gets you out with what you came for.

And then broken as he stumbled.
Albumen softened his frostbit hands every time
he pulled on the gloves they had lain in. Five were stolen.
Three survived in surer hands than his.

Carrying the thin shells back,
tent shredded by wind, boots lost to wind,
stove fueled with the emperors' flensed meat.
Direction blown asunder and the mind's progress in question.

And once returned, once presented to some dry museum clerk,
the one saved egg lay forgotten on an archival shelf, label yellowing.

Every winter he'd look down at his frost-white toes
and think of what they carried, think
of the valley he'd come to, stinking and alive
with the cries of flightless birds that stood, rocked back,
on the sharp bones of their heels.

In Preparation

Explorer, what will you wear? Has someone taken
hair pulled from her brush each morning
since your birth, put it away in a box,
top carved with your name by your father
on the day he thought of your name?
Has she spun the long, fine stuff into thread
then knitted it into socks to warm you?
And the pony your sisters rode, that you,
a boy, harnessed and drove over broken
winter fields, each furrow imagined sastrugi—
has its skin been tanned, cured, and sewn
into mittens?
                        More than your bunk
on the ship, more than the tent pitched on ice,
these will be home to you: layers that hold
your own warmth close, not letting it be lost to air
which itself is not prepared for what your arrival has begun.

II

And what myths would the land write
for itself, were there anyone
to create them who knew
generations of its cold cycles?

When the bearded ones
with pens arrived, there were no
spoken tales to transcribe.

Unless they listened to penguins.
Unless they put ear to the breaking edge.
Unless they felt whalecall through the ship timbers
and then through their own, translatable bones.

On the Longing of Early Explorers

I would prefer one hour of conversation with a native of terra
australis incognita to one with the most learned man in Europe.
—Pierre Louis Moreau de Maupertuis, 1740

Before satellites eyed the earth's whole surface
through the peephole of orbit, before
we all were tracked by numbers trailing from us
like a comet's tail—*O if only*,
they'd say in quaint accents and obscure
sentence structures—if only the unsullied
could be discovered, if only, once found,
it could speak its own nobility and let us
empathize. Poignant, the despair that itched
beneath their powdered wigs, their longing to touch
the unspoiled, their sense that the world was already ruined.

Polar Explorer Nobu Shirase's Five Rules (1911)

1. Never drink hot water

My father a monk, as a boy
all of Konoura knew I was too...
well, they called me naughty.
At the school for priests, they said
Buddhists could not make expeditions.
Too much striving.

2. Never drink alcohol

"A crew of gorillas," "Beasts
of the forest." The locals came
to gawk at our camp in New Zealand,
ground for our huts begged
from a wealthy man. This
after barely scraping funds
to leave Japan? After our small send-off
of only a few bored students? After ice
itself pushed us out of its bays? Drink
might have been permissible.

3. Never drink tea

That is to say, don't be held
hostage to ceremony.
It was one of Mawson's men
who came to our aid. Vouched

for us, told us what he'd seen
of the white land. Scientist
to scientist. I gave him
what had been given me
before I left the templed shore: a sword
made three hundred years ago
by Mutsu no Kami Kaneyasu.
Its maker's name can only be read
on the blade in reflection. What need did I,
a scientist, have of a sword?

4. Do not smoke

We planted our flag on Yamato Yukihara
having marched eight days, unable
to go farther. A week before, Scott
and his men found flags at the spot they sought.
Two weeks before, Amundsen stood on the pole.
These goals are smoke. Our flag
stood on ice unanchored, no land
beneath it to be claimed. Fifty-six years
would pass before another followed
from Japan. My presence by then
only spirit, the evidence sunk. Perhaps
bits of it rising as fog.

5. Never warm your body

Home, debts were larger than the dream
through which they had accrued. I lived
to see the great cloud above two cities,
fire that never should have been made.
A year and a month later, above the fish shop
in Koromo, a blocked intestine killed me.
My farewell poem the only thing left
to show those who found me that once
I'd lived a strange, cold dream.

First Austral Contact

I.

Maybe they were not crazed
but too conservative, their ponderous hulls
sheathed in greenheart, ironwood prows,
mortal ballast of sheep
and brandy, paper and candles.

They couldn't unfurl enough canvas, rig
halyards, booms, and stays enough
to wing up from the white-maned sea and into
the sky's roiled turbulence, and, through that,
to the Sargasso heavens.

II.

Once anchored and off
to trudge the cracking surface,
they were further than ever
from that early hope
of humid land picketed by ice, but
found place alien enough:

The moon's rebounding shine
their winter sun, dogs mad
with the multiplied light, howls
writhing into borealis.

III.

Antarctica's been mapped. There's no oasis
past its metal rind of settlements.

And now white-suited explorers, hoses connected
to fishbowl helmets, have declared
the moon's southern pole
could be scattered with ice, reservoirs
pooled in the explosive sighs
of landing comets.

IV.

What has exploration ever yearned for
but settlement in a new and untried place,

the chance to again make human an eden.

⌐ Notes on Ice in *Bowditch*

ice fog. *Fog composed of suspended particles of ice... it occurs at very low temperatures, and usually in clear, calm weather in high latitudes. The sun is usually visible and may cause halo phenomena.*

Just another texture to stumble through. Another way to lose yourself in water.

ice foot. *A narrow fringe of ice attached to the coast, unmoved by tides and remaining after the fast ice has moved away.*

This is the foot I will place upon your heart. Stubborn and weighty. Unmoved by tides. So long in forming it will outlast nearly anything that would melt it.

ice jam. *An accumulation of broken river ice or sea ice caught in a narrow channel.*

Is that what you call the creaking, popping mass stuck in the thin throat of an argument? Hissing streams rapid around it? Slurry of dislodged bits thick along the banks, rounding sharp corners to rush out and be absorbed?

ice keel. *A downward projecting ridge on the underside of the ice canopy, the counterpart of a ridge. An ice keel may extend as much as 50 meters below sea level.*

Slick. Scraping shoals and giving steerage. I hope I have some deep, sharp thing directing my course, marking the ground I pass over so I can see that I have moved.

Snow Goggles: Whalebone and Sinew

This pair I've carved from the jawbone
of a whale—I don't know what kind—
picked up on a beach of old slaughter.

I chipped and carved the bone, I dug
a narrow trench for light to wash through,
thin flood instead of deluge.

Without them:

       mirage   mirage
          glare unshadowed
       and where the earth's edge flatlines
               mountains of drift in suspension

Last week, sledging, I took them off
and the liquid in my eyes went solid—
I could not close my lids. Stumbledrunk

over floes and chasms, as if darkness
and not light surrounded me.

For several minutes there was no respite
from looking, nothing
to narrow the terrible scape.

Icebound

Another ship trapped in ice, sheathed as ocean
carries on, is carried. The sun gives in
to hours of dusk, dark, dusk.
                              There are mutterings
among the crew. All they want is for their ship
to be a ship. To move where they please it
to move.
              At last someone spots, in a low sun's light,
different air: open water.

In a quarter hour the captain
walks to its edge.
                    But for the ship…

they try and make a path across the ice
of its opposite: ash, soot, shit, dark feathers
pulled from birds skinned for meat,
                                    anything
to draw heat. And with saws and picks
they work down to water.

This goes on for a month. The sea stars
bright on the deep floor return
from a season away.
                    Each day: more soot
& shit & tea leaves hauled. Ice is beaten
from the rigging, the rudder cut free
in case. Beneath them, the ocean carries

on, carries them.
                    At last a man is sick
with the sea's heave, so long unfelt.

The seam they've drawn opens. The crew
tries to remember how to make a course.

Polar Explorer Robert Falcon Scott (1912)

He cried more easily than any man I have ever known.
—Apsley Cherry-Garrard

Each icefall and massif he'd search for a touch
of his sculptress wife's hand. By all reports,
he was a mess. Ambitious and sensitive,
sputtering at each gripe
of his disenchanted crew, and

romantic past all sense. Take,
for example, man-hauling—

While Amundsen slid to the pole
on Nordic skis, the English under Scott

trudged—better to know each jarr, each pound
of need pulled along, better to have felt
the hard accomplishment of each mile. *Ah, Kathleen,*

he thought to his own slogged pace,
you'd be proud. But she was off
flirting with his rival, Nansen, wreaking havoc
with the image of the stoic wife, hungry
for her own adventures.

And when at last he reached the pole he found
another flag, fresh and untattered, waving
the news of his defeat. Then
his doomed march home ... O

think of Shelley lost to suspect drowning, Byron
slain by passion's fever, and then Scott, starving

in his tent eleven miles from cached supplies
he couldn't find.

And now, as I'm telling this, ninety years later,

his body, still wrapped in its reindeer bag, still swaddled
in his tent's frayed silk, flag still tattering, his body
may have reached the Ross Sea
through the slow torrent

of the ice shelf. All the days he plodded,
the land was sliding back beneath him, treadmill
to the sea where he at last is given

a sailor's burial,
maybe today, sunk and drifting.

In Praise of Entropy

In the Dry Valleys, seals lie far
from the shore they'd wandered from,
meat gone to jerky, hide to leather.

Outside Scott's hut at Cape Evans
a mummified husky dog lies, teeth bared,
the leather collar still around its neck.

Inside the hut: a fork on the table,
unrusted. Pages no silverfish or mice will find.
Everything as it was left.

What terror in the cryogenics
of this place, the stasis.

I've lost countless keepsakes—jackknives,
rabbits feet, desperate notes
written in young love. Do we long to see

our pushed-away meals still on the table,
lost tempers still in the air?
This is why we gape:

that we might return to a world
which lets us forget what we've abandoned.

Arctos/Antarktikos

The Greeks were right.
The land beneath the pole star

toward which the great bear
noses his bright stars,

never hiding that constant
and fruitless work, is mirrored.

Take this, then, as proof
that imagination is not useless.

Or as a sign that truth
will circle through our traceries.

Back before the myths were spoken
all land was lumped

on one side of the globe
like an aching tooth, there was ocean

above both poles. Then the slow spread
of earth's humors: Asia, India, Australia,

all the soft-voweled continents drifting.
And in this present

which is long enough to call fact,
the Greeks—fathers of Western

Civilization as taught at least in my
grade school—were right. Two white

lands. And the stars were right: bears
circling the northern one, gyres

of flesh and need. And in the southern
sky, abstract and tricky, Octans. The octant.

Old instrument telling sailors
how much calculation is required

when fumbling unintuitive lands.

En Route

They prepared as they could: reinforcing
pants or bonding with dogs, fiddling
with tent design or sleeping bag hoods.

It was a work of the imagination. It was
fortune-tellers' work. Different qualities
of sun. Different qualities of wind. I hear

that in Madeira they pulled out
the sledges and ran them down
cobbled streets. It's not as if confetti

prompted them, made for them a blizzard.
They were bored. Ready. And still
so many miles to go before genius
and blunder could be proved.

Polar Explorer Frank Hurley, Photographer on Shackleton's *Endurance* Expedition (1915)

One by one he lay the glass negatives on ice
and squinted through their reversals. This one,
saved aside to be soldered into its tin box.
This one, smashed on the hard, white ground,
misgivings and reconsiderations
scattered and winking.

Yesterday, he'd broken into the cracking hull,
plunged shirtless into the slushy hold and fished out
what he could, heaved it up
                              onto the ice as Shackleton
tossed a gold watch, gold lighter, gold coins
onto the fissured surface before the makeshift camp,
telling the men they could take only two pounds
of unnecessary attachment from here. All of them

left something behind. But there, on the ground
that clenched and crushed their ship, they declared
what mattered most: silver nitrate
                          lyrics, spoken light.
                                    He made shards
of some 400 plates then packed a few reels of motion
film, prints already made, and the 120 negatives left unbroken.

His to trudge and huddle with nearly half a year
on the ice shelf, to stuff into the dory's bow
that pitched him for a week, to wait with
for rescue five months on Elephant Island.

He filmed the ship breaking, left the Prestwich No. 5
in its stand, slipped a small Kodak into his pocket
with thirty-eight more chances to curate what history
would be made in the unmapped time before him.

I don't know how much what he left on ice weighed
—broken glass, lenses, bellows stand, plate still camera, tripods—
or how heavy were the things he saved.

Has there ever been a better measure
of hope's precise and illogical weight?

Song of the Ice Breaker Prow

Too soft, the waves, too soft
the rogues and breakers,
my grain pulled tight
at the tree's cut core

and eager now to fight
as axe and adze gored
me. Raise steam, boys,
raise steam. We'll force her

through the lead. The sea
stretches acres,
white and cracked,
a crust I'm made

to break like bread. I've crashed
floes thicker than a horse's
chest, pushed
aside challengers

to my strong stem, forced
myself through as knife, ravager,
again and again into my own deepening mark.

Polar Explorer Ernest Shackleton (1922)

There are a few things, sounds mostly, that stay in the mind,
repeating.

Home after the rescue, his wrecked ship flickered twice daily
on a London screen to his own voiced accompaniment.

We all have unexplained rhythms
and echoes inside the still-mysterious landscape
of our chests. The heart's slight variations of *tick* and *tock*.

That smooth ticking of reels, regular
            and anticipated, unlike
the unrhythmed slap of halyards or
of the snap of a hull's planks and ribs
                        within a clench of ice.

But not unlike the evening rattle, part of his boyhood
clocking, within the dark purse
of his father's medical bag, steel
and mysterious vials.
                        And not unlike
the more steady chronometer
hung against his captain's chest
throughout their legendary, unsteady ride
that he keeps, at the climax of the film's narration, retelling
before lights, applause, check handed to him in the wings.

            Other sounds associate. The octet rustle
of his sisters' skirts now linked to mountain slope glissade, a fall
and arrival that made him hero.

                              And, tied to that,
the sad, aluminum rush of fertilizer
into a ship's filling hold, his penultimate career.

                    An unsurprising return, then,
              once his fame wound down.
        An attempt to recoil the clock spring,
to begin another sequence of its gears.

The landmarks of his triumph
resighted, each bleak one called out
to the crew that he could gather, his breath
again falling from his lips as ice, he allowed his heart
to stop.

        And just before that beat, in
the silence between the one before and
the last,
              he remembered that during the long slide
              toward rescue and fame
years ago, in that unchecked descent of unreasonable glee,
his captain forgot to hold their timepiece
to his chest, letting it bounce and jerk at the cord around his neck and,
at one point, the steady chronometer flew out before him, all
jeweled wheels and unnecessary, grinning cogs.

Fine-Tuning

First overwintering. First
foot on the coast, leopard seal shot,
whale oil rendered, man gone mad.
Anne, snowshoeing
above treeline just after fresh
powder had topped the peaks, ran down a slope
shouting with each step *First!*
First! First! Snow kicking up, the mark
of her tracks deep and, it's true
from what we could see, first.
Of course she wasn't. They weren't.
Until we narrowed the categories
sufficiently: first woman since
last snowfall to set foot here.
First time I have felt dismay
since the last time I dismissed it.

Notes on Ice in *Bowditch*

ice limit. *The climatological term referring to the extreme minimum or extreme maximum extent of the ice edge in any given month or period based on observations over a number of years. The term should be preceded by minimum or maximum as appropriate.*

The definition excludes nothing. It can always be expanded. You can always fall further in love. You can always find love more impossible.

ice needle. *A long, thin ice crystal whose cross-section is typically hexagonal.*

Darn my shirts with this, please. Pull strings of frozen stuff through the cloth with it. I want ice to be my mending. I want cold to stitch me.

ice of land origin. *Ice formed on land or in an ice shelf, found floating in water, including ice that is stranded or grounded.*

Until you're all water, the origins still count. Disguises and relocations aren't that successful. And if melt is the end of it? Well, what shore do you think you'll wash up on first?

ice patch. *An area of pack ice less than 5.4 nautical miles across.*

Again the sewing of the ocean up with frozen water, and I'll admit that ice can look like cloth, slightly rumpled, the herringbone of flakes patterning its weave. Its mending is all about a falling off of heat. Let the argument cool so that we can walk across it, stand safely on the thin surface between what once were floes.

Polar Explorer Louise Arner Boyd (1924)

What on that Spitsbergen boat captured her
even as she retched into brash ice
that played the hull like a snare? The biographer

calls what she saw "the love of her life." Mirage
is common in northern seas. It's true, she never married
but lived with Greenland as hearth and lodestone,

trudging the shores in winter, summer, lugging
huge cameras to map the land in detail
not granted the maps before. I've not read she was frigid.

California socialite turned explorer, sailor-
tongued, nose powdered each morning before
she went up on deck. First woman to set foot

on Fraz-Joseph Land. Snug in quiviut
jacket, sweater, and muffler. First woman
to fly over the pole. And, come WWII,

her pictures strategic to the effort. Obsession,
this once and at last, turned asset. Mostly, though,
I imagine her on that first boat not her own. I think

of the captain hauling tourists out over grounds
he once hunted or fished, bored with the day tour,
with the awe, the tame introduction to seas

he'd worked all seasons. She's ignorant of him, in love
with her own thrum to the air, the ice, the impossible
walrus. She senses her life's compass

has just set its pointed foot and the rest of her years
will rotate around it. He may have noticed her
sighing over the rail, shoving her dreams

out over the ice. Most likely he didn't, thinking
of home, of his love or hatred for the sea and what
he'd come to, a shuttle for fantasies

that, every so often, survived the trip home,
the docking, the littered wharf, whether he knew it or not.
Whether he cared or not. Either way, he brought

the boat to the pier, moored her, and, after the tourists left,
tended bilge and logbook, checked the planking,

prepared for the next day out in the shifting ice,
the fertile seas that he, too, knew.

Roughnecks and Rakes One and All, the Poet Speaks to Her Subjects, Polar Explorers

I won't write you that voice,
piggy, crass
forged by salt &
cold & isolation.
Filed to edge
by time-wrung,
absence-wrought rasping
or, if not those,
by what made you endure.

I know we're
bad luck on boats,
women, worse
on ice, too humid
for this hoar.
And you hate my pen
tracking through
your stories. But

I write you,
and that's what love you get,
meted out, doled like rum.
Through line and vowel, my
voice chooses
yours, forced
by yours.

I'd like to say
local deviations
make this
true enough
triangulation
for polar work,

that despite my distance
and the tendency of light
over ice toward mirage,
some shape comes through
that both of us
can recognize.

Polar Explorer Donald B. MacMillan Brings Color Film to the Arctic (1925)

Grease ice melon with algae, claret floes of pupping grounds:
from the beginning, one man on every venture
was issued brush and paint to translate
what the strange sky
    —colors shifting in each breeze—
pressed against his iris.

But they had no palette, no dialect
to describe the shawled earth. No *aniu*
(snow on ground) or *muraneq* (soft deep
snow). No *qanisqineq* (snow floating
on water) or *utvak* (snow carved in block).
No hundred words. In time, though,

use and hue began to build a lexicon:
crevasses descend blue and haunting, avoid their quick release;
when honey smears the bergs at waterline, rich ground for hunting;
pink in the petals of ice flowers, time to think again of home

where description of that long and foreign cold
will be doubted. The red-swept sky, the minarets
of ice, the blushing snow received not
as what was seen, but what had been envisioned
by men made mad. MacMillan thought

he'd found his proof, but even Technicolor's
objectivity, once home, seemed static, framed,
absurd—chemicals warped, no doubt, by conditions
beyond what they were made for.

No lens yet can speak the vision
of the overwhelmed eye at the time
of seeing. I will never know
what they hoped to see,
what the vast light allowed them.

Wives of the Polar Explorers

Some hunk of ice or rock named after them, an address,
a memory for the men to write to those cold months, adding
to the pages then carrying them home.

Adélie d'Urville

The send-off is where she's most familiar, starched
petticoats at dockside attempting to empathize
with the ice-filled, cracking sea

Eva Nansen

her husband's headed for. *Good-bye, dear heart—if*
you lose a finger, string it for me as a charm
to beckon you home. Lucky if she

Kathleen Scott

has a fortune's backing because what bills
could the cold freight, the new maps,
the slim discoveries and rough ventures pay?

Josephine Peary

In the swelling absence, often,
a child born with his nose, his
remembered mouth. Of course

Lucy Henson

the return was worse. His restless, frostbit
limp, his early-aged eyes unable to focus
in the temperate air, his immediate schemes

Emily Shackleton

to leave again—or the household inspected
and the crew found wanting, his command
chafing. It could go either way.

Elizabeth Byrd

Either way, no easy slide back
into a shared sleep. *I missed you, I missed
you* each would say, trying to understand

Liz Bradfield

through the strange dialects discovered in separation
of solitude, of companionship.

Polar Explorer Richard Evelyn Byrd (1933)

Among the things he brought to his constructed ordeal: 2 reams
of paper, 3 dozen pencils, 2 packets of tooth picks, 2 mirrors.

Smooth-faced, a petulance to his lips,
blue eyes slightly bulged with anxious striving and the sense
that he's too late for great acclaim. Starched uniform
splayed across his chest, white as the continent itself.

And so that winter in the hut did clothe him,
its chill blanket, its slim light, its solitude,
its deranged skies.

That sterile Walden and its failures.

What he had forgotten: cookbook (later found)
and alarm clock.

Struggling outside to muse
upon the universe's clockwork. Faint in his bunk
from the stove chimney's poisoning fumes—
a makeshift, leaky thing
of tin cans. Detailing in his valiant journal
how a navy man keeps despair at bay, lives through pain
with a stoic sense of poetry, avoids
the greedy sleep of phenobarbital,
the lure of rescue.

Some trials seem contrived
for the weight of accolades they'll bring.
Their passage loud with anticipated medals, applause.

Some books he read (in order of his own selecting):
Of Human Bondage, Soliloquies in England, Scott's
diary (grim hero), *Life of Alexander, Theory of the Leisure
Class, Heloise & Abelard, All
the Brothers Were Valiant* (all of them, he was relieved
to read), *The House* (when he was most sick,
even the radio crank too much
to manage) *of Exile*.

Important facts: once, when he was well,
ice sealed the cabin door and he was stuck inside; once,
taking a small walk, his leg pushed through a thin
bit of ice and the fall below was deeper
than his flashlight's beam;
once, when weak with monoxide, the door
sealed him outside for almost long enough;

and once, worst of all, adrift in a white haze
of his own making, daydreaming,
he wandered beyond the little flags
that led toward home.

He was lost. And not one distant peak, not one white swirl,
not one green flicker in the emotive sky cared.

WYSSA

—Antarctica, 1961

Compressed for Morse, compressed to better the odds
this first, flimsy signal might send sense across ocean
unbroken, I type just WYSSA, which you know means
All my love darling in this telegraph of foreseen
longing. In further news, YIHKE—*I have grown*

a beard which is generally admired and with it
will tease the soft hollow between your hip bones
as you lie in the green field beyond our gate or,
if you dislike the beard, I will lay my head in your lap
and let you cut it from me, cut away my months gone

and burn them, acrid and bitter. WUYGT—*elephant seals*
are breeding, and although their heaving is nothing like
our shadows against cabbage-rose wallpaper, I am
aroused. They are the only flesh here, and they slap
against each other with unrelenting fervor. YOGIP—

please send details of bank account. Do you have
enough? Has my time here at least fattened something?
Can I afford to say WYSSA again? YAYIR—*fine snow*
has penetrated through small crevices in the buildings.
I am cold. And although we decided this code

with your breath still against my neck, your heat
anything but distant, believe that my heart's capacity
has, if anything, expanded in this chill. YONOY—
from now on, all I hammer against the sounding metal
of this small machine is WYSSA. All of it.

Notes on Ice in *Bowditch*

ice rind. *A brittle shiny crust of ice formed on a quiet surface by direct freezing or from grease ice, usually in water of low salinity. Of thickness to about 5 centimeters, ice rind is easily broken by wind or swell, commonly breaking into rectangular pieces.*

I guess we always knew that the world was a fruit, rinded. But what doesn't have a skin that can be peeled? Me, the morning's dim wakening, our house's shell. Anything can be broken to the pulp of its heart.

ice sheet. *Continuous ice overlaying a large land area.*

Draw that up to your chin in the night, the music of it breaking, your feet dim hillocks near the horizon of the bed. Lay that sheet, freshly laundered with new snow, over a clothesline, unsnapping in the breeze, pulling the line, the branch it's tied to, pulling it all into contact with the earth.

ice shelf. *A floating ice sheet attached to the coast and of considerable thickness, showing 20 to 50 meters or more above sea level. Usually of great horizontal extent and with a level or gently undulating surface, the ice shelf is augmented by annual snow accumulation and often by the seaward extension of land glaciers. Limited areas of the ice shelf may be aground.*

It's these points of contact that matter, frozen teeth biting down toward sand or mud or whatever lies across the surface of the earth. What conversation of scrapes and bumps, of digging and crumbling, must take place there, at the deeply hidden joining of earth and freeze, water flowing around and occasionally between them. The cold knocking for entrance to the earth's hot core.

Amundsen in Nome

His head is huge, bronze, snow
drift in the eye sockets, and set
near the spruce-burl arch that now
marks the end of the Iditarod—

annual cameras and bright fabric, politicians
sitting on sleds with mushers above,
both crossing into the next day's news as they pass
the site that honors Amundsen's
chronicled arrival:

props spinning a silver abdomen of hydrogen
over what had never been overflown—
the globe's cap.

                Ski to ship to Zeppelin.
He had to like the ease, no shelter to pitch
and stow daily, no salt in the water casks
or animals to tend. A new danger
—headwinds, ice fog, fire—could always

present itself, and he explored that
as much as the nature of pack ice,
the many uses of seal. As much how
as whether, as much new
as done.

On Ground Tracked by Wolf, Snowshoe, Sled, Ski, and Snowmachine

Which romance? That's the question because
romance lies thicker than permafrost here. Choose

the shoe-leather-eating Franklin. Choose Bering's
wise and unloved Steller, plucking sandwort

from the shores to stave off scurvy. Choose the
Dorset of the East: igloos and umiaks. Basque

whalers. Cod fishermen. The Aleut or
Athabascan. Bush pilots. Dog race of penicillin

from Seward to Nome. Or the attempted and
attempted forays for the Northwest Passage. Or go

pre-historic toward Beringia: beavers weighing in
at four hundred pounds, mastadons, the giant short-faced

bear. Pipeline or kayak. Or both or both—the
loud and clashing songs of them all, like

the North Slope in late June: so many birds
that clamor becomes not something to pick

through for individual song, but a fact itself.
A wall of noise under a sky so long-lit

that, above territory, defense, or hunger, it cries
its own capacity to hold each contradictory note.

Polar Explorer John Forbes Nash, Jr.,
Self-Declared Emperor of Antarctica (1967)

He's a genius mathematician and insane
which goes a long way to explain it.

But why hadn't I thought of this
before? That someone might
want a throne there, ruler
of most of the world's fresh water,

inaccessible. Penguins his uncomplicated subjects, little history
to surmount, and the ground's own pure and endless
fractal variations—or permutations as it's all
a rearranging of Hydrogen, Oxygen, Hydrogen—of white.

A land to quiet his mind's static, a slate
for his huge equations, numbers scrawled across
the faint sense of what was once expected there—tropics
at the pole, Eve's descendants picnicking together, no apple
bit and abandoned on the ground, no snake, Adam not
fingering the soft arch of his lost rib—
logic overwriting myth.

Coastline unmappable. Falling and
rebuilding. Lost and unlost.

And the katabatic wind to howl out
any unwanted groan nag whine
mumble screech whimper.
To overwhelm the clamor
of his own dissonance.

But the heart of anything, at last,
is only conquerable as long
as supplies hold out.
Brief forays and then

open   wild   white

Why Shackleton's Stories Are Being Retold in Book and Film

We are all wondering the same things
in this darkened room, the ship not enduring
after all, the men enduring *despite*:
How do the trials of our lives compare?

What would Shackleton have done
when the baby didn't stop crying. What
would he have done if his credit cards
were all denied or his girlfriend
slept with his brother or if he was downsized?

And would we have survived, too, if
given a chance? Kept peace and sanity
and most of our toes? Kept hope
when cell phone, wristwatch, and film advance failed and
borealis was the only electric thing within range?

Lady: Polar Explorer and Last
of the Enderby Island Cattle (1993)

We made her twice, first
through displacement and neglect,
then through vial and biotech nudge.

For over a century, her Shetland short-horn kin
ranged sub-Antarctic Enderby Island, endured
its winds, found forage in what
was cast to shore. And so, as they
changed the island, it changed them.

Like bilge-brought zebra mussels
in the Great Lakes, like Aleutian
bird-egg-eating foxes. Like the dream
of the huia or woolly mammoth roaming again.

On Enderby, Lady worked her cud of seaweed, she
hoofed down the native flora, and times changed.

State-paid shooters took out
all forty-seven head. They took
eight hundred straws of semen,
but the herd, the breed was thought lost.

One year later, two men found
Lady's hoofprints, tracked her,
netted her, brought her to
New Zealand where

22 embryos reconstructed with
meataphase II cytoplasts and quiescent
cells were activated and fused

and two calves were born, and one, our Elsie
(LC, Lady Clone), survived, nuzzling the teat
that is her mother's, her own, the brine milk.

Still, I want to know a few things: If
something differs in the gaze of Lady
and her clone. If wind sounds
the same through their identical ears. If seaweed
on the tongue speaks of something lost.
If what was done was good.

They Called it Nukey-Poo

Ten years of fission on the flank of Erebus.
The name seems warning enough. Now add

the steam from its crater, the melted snow
in that deep bowl. You'd think that they'd
think twice. But it was 1962. Power

from the cute twirl of atoms seemed clean
as a Kandinsky. Nukey-Poo humming along.
No growl of generator. No diesel fumes.

In the seventies it went to shit.
Leakage on the hillside.

And what then to do with the thirteen thousand
tons of waste? What's done with any casualty.
Ship it home. Bury it. Mark carefully the grave.

ice storm. A storm characterized by a fall of freezing precipitation with significant buildup of ice on exposed surfaces.

Cleat, halyard, shoelace, earlobe, shank, capstan. All covered. This is when we see freezing at its most voracious. This is when the ice becomes more than weather but a greed we understand.

ice stream. The part of an inland ice sheet in which the ice flows more rapidly and not necessarily in the same direction as the surrounding ice. The margins are sometimes clearly marked by a change in direction of the surface slope, but may be indistinct.

Are you so sure of the difference between freeze and thaw? One is not necessarily moving toward the other. Always a place between that is flowing and hard to define. This is why apologies are difficult.

ice under pressure. Ice in which deformation processes are actively occurring; hence the ice is a potential impediment or danger to shipping.

Active deformation. Sure, that's what happens under pressure, though I'd not have thought up the turn of phrase myself. But I like it. As if I'm working at some new juxtaposition, as if I've got a hand in the reordering, as if I could choose the deformation for me.

ice-worn. Abraded by ice.

You may feel this one acutely, here at the end of this glossary. Me? I'm polished, not worn, glossy after the passage of tons of ice across me, the stone of my heart buffed to a sheen. Scoured. Ready for love to find a new foothold on me.

Vicarious

You're not worried
about frostbite, snow
glare, or crevasse. Not
about a leopard seal
beneath the ice you walk,
stalking. Not madness.

It's the passage between—
two days of retching
each way, Ushuia to Antarctica
and back.

I've read so many stories
about what got them,
the explorers, the sailors,
the sealers and adventurers.
But this is you. Whose breath
I've heard change from dream
for ten years of mornings.

You travel to my fascination
and I am full of envy. You do not
see for me, hear for me. It doesn't work
like that. You see. And it will
be different from books, from my
imaginings. There will be no putting aside

when you're tired of ice and all
the awe that it assumes. And no

convenient editing. Oil cans on the beach.
Footsteps and footsteps from the common
landings where you'll land and walk
your guests, pointing out, comprehending,
marrying what you know to what you see
and all it tells of knowing's impossibility.

Polar Explorer Lynne Cox (2002)

I have tasted the globe's varying brine, the specific
tangs of plankton banding its shores. I have thrown
my body in, no wet suit, no shark cage.
> 1971: Catalina Channel. 27 miles. 12 hours,
> 36 minutes. Age 14.

Abstracts about my body tell of its neutral
buoyancy, the statistically significant temperature
of my core, measured one year in a cold jacuzzi,
thermometer up my ass.
> 1972: Record crossing of the English Channel. 27 miles.
> 9 hours, 57 minutes.
> 1973: Record crossing of the English Channel. 33 miles.
> 9 hours, 36 minutes.

Sailors have always feared water, placed all faith
in the bellied hull—to abandon boat for sea
a breach of trust, a crack in the planking.
> 1976: First to cross the Straits of Magellan. 4.5 miles. 42° F.

Let me show you how I swim in rough seas,
head up to conserve heat, feet barely fluttering.
Let me show you the goggles I wore in the Gulf of Aqaba.
The world has not been explored until ...
> 1979: Cape of Good Hope. 10 miles. 70° F.

watch me flail into the current—am I crossing
a time zone, a lexeme, a date line,
a hemisphere now? Now?
> 1980: Around the island of Joga Shima.

Drive me there. Let me slip from the fantail
and swim with what in the water is not liquid—
sea lion, brash ice, trawl net—did any of us
really want to be human?

1987: Little Diomede to Big Diomede. First to cross
    the Bering Strait. Toasted by Reagan and Gorbachev.
    2 hours, 16 minutes. Age 30.
I promise, before my prime is up, before I become
coach, figurehead, emcee I will push
the heat of my heart through even the coldest sea.
    1990: Across the Beagle Channel between Chile and Argentina.
Trails of bubbles from penguins
traveling at four times my speed.
Water sweet with glacial runoff.
    2002: 1.22 miles in Neko Harbor. First to swim to Antarctica's
    shore. 25 minutes. 33° F. Age 45.
How I hate the thoughtlessness of breath on land, the arms
that pull me to my awkward vertical,
the language anchored
—even here—
to the wet shore.

Notes

"A Grim Place for Ponies: South Pole Expedition, 1910": Italicized phrases are from Apsley Cherry-Garrard's *The Worst Journey in the World*.

"Wilson's Specimens": Dr. E.A. Wilson was the doctor and zoologist on Scott's fatal Terra Nova expedition and one of the South Pole Party who never returned.

"Notes on Ice in *Bowditch*": *Bowditch* is the familiar term for Nathanial Bowditch's classic *The American Practical Navigator*, first published in 1802 and still in print and in use today. The definitions of ice forms are from the book's glossary.

"Polar Explorer Jules Sébastien César Dumont d'Urville (1840)": Italicized phrases are taken from *Two Voyages to the South Seas* and *Antarctica: The Complete Story*. It is indeed the Venus de Milo that he took from Greece.

"Invention": Italicized phrase from Edgeworth David, as recorded in Bernadette Hince's *Antarctic Dictionary*.

"Legacy": The form of this poem was inspired by "Ramblin' on My Mind" by Diana Blakely, *Best American Poetry 2003*.

"Polar Explorer Robert Falcon Scott (1912)": Epigraph taken from *The Worst Journey in the World*.

"In Praise of Entropy": The italicized stanza is taken from *A for Antarctica: Facts and Stories from the Frozen South*. Since writing this poem, there has been concern expressed that warming temperatures will bring increased humidity to Antarctica, thus introducing rot.

"Polar Explorer Richard Evelyn Byrd (1933)": Details taken from Byrd's own account of his time in Antarctica, *Alone*.

"WYSSA": The capitalized letter groupings and italicized phrases are taken from Bently code, which was used by Australian researchers in Antarctica from 1954 through the 1980s to avoid radio signal disruptions caused by various polar phenomenon.

"Amundsen in Nome:" Amundsen has many polar accomplishments to his name: first to the south pole, first to reach *both* the north and south poles. His airship venture aboard the *Norge* came late in life. Two years later, in 1928, he disappeared in a rescue mission to the Arctic.

"Polar Explorer John Forbes Nash, Jr. Self-Declared Emperor of Antarctica (1967)": Nash entered the popular culture briefly via the film "A Beautiful Mind."

Bibliography

Because so much of this book comes from books, from reading about and thereby trying to inhabit the Arctic and Antarctica, I feel I must credit a few sources. There are shelves of books about the poles, either first-hand accounts from explorers or later biographies and texts. The few below were, for me, particularly inspiring:

Bowditch, Nathaniel. *The American Practical Navigator.* Everything you want to know about what a sailor is supposed to know. Often put in unintentionally charming language. The entry on the sewing machine is one of my favorites.

Byrd, Admiral Richard E. *Alone.* Afterword by David G. Campbell. This reproduction of Byrd's 1938 account of his Austral winter alone in a hut is a fascinating read. Byrd is an unwittingly unreliable narrator of his own tale.

Cherry-Garrard, Apsley. *The Worst Journey in the World.* First published in 1922, Cherry-Garrard's account of Sir Robert Falcon Scott's last (and doomed) expedition to the South Pole is a classic. This long book is sensitively written, full of wonder, questioning, horror, and tenuous hope.

Henson, Matthew. *A Black Explorer at the North Pole.* Henson sets the record straight about his role in Peary's expedition, keeping a firmly chipper, breezy tone throughout.

Hince, Bernadette. *Antarctic Dictionary.* In the spirit of the *Oxford English Dictionary,* Hince includes quotations that show where various polar-related terms come from and how they were (and are) used. For a place with no language of its own, Antarctica has collected quite a unique vocabulary.

Lansing, Alfred. *Endurance.* Lansing writes a straightforward adventure narrative of Shackleton's crew trapped in the Antarctic pack ice in 1914. It was sitting and reading this book about fifteen years ago that, for me, kicked off this obsession with polar exploration.

Lopez, Barry. *Arctic Dreams.* An inspirational classic that ranges the north. I remember sneaking pages of this book as a deckhand on day tour boats in Puget Sound, dreaming of bigger water.

McGonigal, David and Dr. Lynn Woodworth. *Antarctica: The Complete Story.* A premiere volume for those interested in Antarctica, this book presents information on people, places, and animals associated with the white continent.

Acknowledgments

The following poems appeared, sometimes in earlier versions, in the journals listed below. Many thanks to the editors for their support and encouragement.

Alaska Quarterly Review: "Polar Explorer Robert Falcon Scott (1912)," "Amundsen in Nome"

The Anchorage Daily News: "Polar Explorer Frank Hurley, Photographer on Shackleton's Endurance Expedition (1915)"

The Atlantic Monthly: "WYSSA"

Blackbird: "Snow Goggles: Whalebone and Sinew," "Polar Explorer Salomon August Andrée (1897)"

The Cream City Review: "Polar Explorer Capt. John Cleves Symmes (1820)," "Polar Explorer Donald B. MacMillan Brings Color Film to the Arctic (1925)"

Ecotone: "Arctos/Antarctikos"

Epoch: "Polar Explorer Apsley Cherry-Garrard (1911)"

Field: "Wilson's Specimens," "The Third Reich Claims Neu Schwabenland"

The Gay and Lesbian Review: "On the Longing of Early Explorers"

Ice-Floe: International Poetry of the Far North: "The First Explorers Thought Eden Lay Beyond Antarctica" (here the prelude to the book)

The Iowa Review: "Polar Explorer: Nobu Shirase's Five Rules (1911)"

Lumberyard: "In Praise of Entropy"

Mantis: "In the Polar Regions"

Many Mountains Moving: "Polar Explorer John Forbes Nash, Jr. Self-Declared Emperor of Antarctica (1967)"

Ocho: "Fine-Tuning," "Why Shackleton's Stories Are Being Retold in Book and Film"

Ploughshares: "Phrenology"

Poetry: "Against Solitude"

Radical Society: "Legacy," "Polar Explorer: Matthew Henson, Assistant to Admiral Peary (1909)"

Rhino: "Why They Went"

So To Speak: "Polar Explorer: Lynne Cox (2002)"

Virginia Quarterly Review: "Polar Explorer: Adrien de Gerlache, First to Winter Below the Antarctic Circle (1898)"

The following poems appear in the *From the Fishouse* archive (www.fishousepoems.org): "prelude," "Thoughts on Early Arctic Explorers and Your Time in Churchill," "Polar Explorer Jules Sébastien César Dumont d'Urville (1840)," "The Third Reich Claims Neu Schwabenland," "Polar Explorer Matthew Henson, Assistant to Admiral Peary (1909)," "Against Solitude," "Roughnecks and Rakes One and All, the Poet Speaks to Her Subjects, Polar Explorers," "WYSSA"

A Wallace Stegner Fellowship, a fellowship at the Vermont Studio Center, and a scholarship at the Bread Loaf Writer's Conference enriched the poems of this book.

My thanks go out to the friends, mentors, and colleagues I call on in a pinch (literary, existential, or practical) and to celebrate: Linda Bierds, Eavan Boland, Nickole Brown, Christine Byl, Stacie Cassarino, Amy Crawford, Douglas Culhane, Sara Dietzman, Jonathan Fink, Amy Groshek, Eloise Klein Healy, Sean Hill, S. Lochlann Jain, Rebecca King, Scott Landry, Amy Mandel, Linda McCarriston, Katina Rodis, Eva Saulitis, the Schmidts one and all, Raina Stefani, Alexandra Teague, Mark Temelko, Gabriel Travis, Joshua Tyree, Sarah Van Sanden, GC Waldrep, and all my fellow Stegner fellows. Special thanks to Gabriel Fried for his belief in the book and his fierce eye.

I owe much to my family– parents, grandmother, and sisters—for their incredible support.

Finally, Lisa. I'd have been obsessed with the subject without you, but you gave it warmth.

Elizabeth Bradfield (www.ebradfield.com) is the author of a previous collection, *Interpretive Work*, winner of the Audre Lorde Prize and a finalist for a Lambda Literary Award. Her poems have appeared in the *Atlantic Monthly*, *Poetry*, and many other publications. She is founder and co-editor of Broadsided Press, as well as a naturalist who has worked in Alaska, the Eastern Canadian Arctic and elsewhere. A recent Wallace Stegner Fellow at Stanford University, she now lives on Cape Cod.